DO NOT REMOVE
CARDS FROM POCKET

WHAT IS A
SHOOTING
STAR?

BY ISAAC ASIMOV

Gareth Stevens Children's Books
MILWAUKEE

For a free color catalog describing Gareth Stevens' list of high-quality children's books, call 1-800-341-3569 (USA) or 1-800-461-9120 (Canada).

For their help in the preparation of *Ask Isaac Asimov: What Is a Shooting Star?*, the editors and designers gratefully thank Max Knowlton-Sachner, Norah Knowlton-Sachner, Dominic Wyman, and Cheray Wyman. Special thanks also to the Milwaukee Public Museum for loaning specimens from its collection for photographic purposes.

Library of Congress Cataloging-in-Publication Data

Asimov, Isaac, 1920-
    What is a shooting star? / by Isaac Asimov. — A Gareth Stevens Children's Books ed.
       p. cm. — (Ask Isaac Asimov)
    Includes bibliographical references and index.
    Summary: Explains the nature of meteors or "shooting stars" and how they are different from real stars.
    ISBN 0-8368-0436-8
    1. Meteors—Juvenile literature. [1. Meteors.] I. Title. II. Series: Asimov, Isaac, 1920- Ask Isaac Asimov.
QB751.5.A85 1991
523.5'1—dc20   90-25922

A Gareth Stevens Children's Books edition

Edited, designed, and produced by
Gareth Stevens Children's Books
1555 North RiverCenter Drive, Suite 201
Milwaukee, Wisconsin 53212, USA

Picture Credits
pp. 2-3, Paul Dimare; pp. 4-5, Rick Karpinski/DeWalt and Associates; pp. 6-7, © Frank Zullo; pp. 8-9, Paul Dimare; pp. 10-11, John Sanford/Science Photo Library; pp. 10-11 (border), courtesy of NASA; pp. 12-13, © Gareth Stevens, Inc.; p. 14 (inset), © Edward J. Olsen; pp. 14-15, Mark Maxwell; pp. 16-17, Mary Evans Picture Library; pp. 18-19, Frank Zullo, © 1986; p. 20, Mark Mille/DeWalt and Associates; p. 21, © Gareth Stevens, Inc.; pp. 22-24, Rick Karpinski/DeWalt and Associates

Cover illustration, Paul Dimare: An artist's rendition of a meteor falling through Earth's atmosphere. People on the ground might see this meteor as a shooting star streaking across the night sky.

Series editor: Elizabeth Kaplan
Editor: Patricia Lantier-Sampon
Series designer: Sabine Huschke
Picture researcher: Daniel Helminak
Picture research assistant: Diane Laska
Consulting editor: Matthew Groshek

Printed in MEXICO

1 2 3 4 5 6 7 8 9 97 96 95 94 93 92 91

Contents

A World of Questions 4
Blazing Streaks of Light 7
Catch a Falling Star 8
Craters = Rough Sledding 10
Rock or Meteorite? 12
Danger — Cosmic Blasting Zone 14
Clouds of Dust 17
Watch the Stars, See How They Fall............18
Shooting Stars — Stars That Aren't Stars 21
The Mysteries of Meteors 22

More Books to Read 23
Places to Write 23
Glossary 23
Index 24

Words that appear in the glossary are printed in **boldface** type the
first time they occur in the text.

A World of Questions

Our world is full of strange and beautiful things. The night sky glimmers with **stars**. Lightning flashes from dark clouds during a thunderstorm. Sometimes we have questions about things we see. Asking questions helps us appreciate the wonders of the Universe.

For instance, have you ever seen a shooting star? Look at the sky on a dark, clear night, and you may see a star moving across the sky. This is a shooting star. It may also be called a "falling star." But is it really a star? Does it really fall? Let's find out.

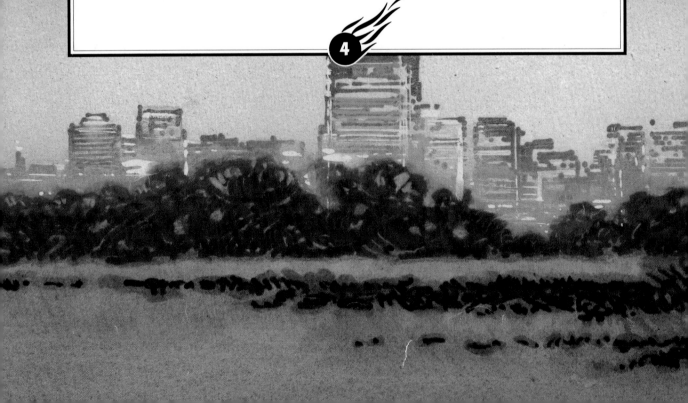

Blazing Streaks of Light

A shooting star is not just a point of light as other stars are. A shooting star looks like a streak of light, as shown to the left. It flashes across the sky and then disappears. Toward the end, it may get brighter. In rare cases, it may explode. Most of the time, it just fades after a second or two.

After the shooting star is gone, all the ordinary stars still remain in the sky. No matter how many shooting stars you see, the ordinary stars do not disappear.

Catch a Falling Star

A shooting star isn't a real star. It is a piece of rock zooming through Earth's **atmosphere**. Its motion through the air heats it white hot. That's why it makes a glowing streak. Scientists call such a rock a **meteor**.

Most meteors are about the size of a piece of dust. They burn up completely in the air above the Earth. A few meteors are so large that they don't burn up. What's left of the meteor hits the ground. A meteor that hits the ground is called a **meteorite**.

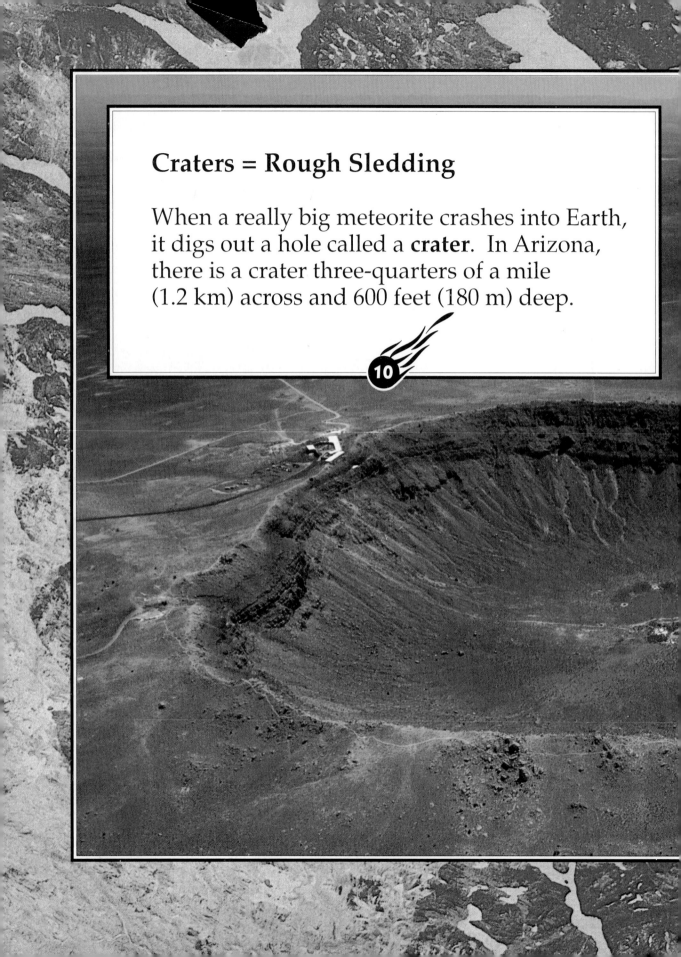

Craters = Rough Sledding

When a really big meteorite crashes into Earth, it digs out a hole called a **crater**. In Arizona, there is a crater three-quarters of a mile (1.2 km) across and 600 feet (180 m) deep.

10

We don't find many craters on Earth. Most craters here have been overgrown by plants or worn away by wind and rain. Craters are common, however, on the Moon and on Mercury. On these worlds with no wind, rain, or life, craters last for billions of years.

11

Rock or Meteorite?

People sometimes find meteorites after they fall. Most meteorites are made of rock. These meteorites, including the one above, look a lot like rocks on Earth. A meteorite is hard to identify unless you actually see one fall or hear it hit the ground. A few meteorites are made mainly of metals, such as **iron** and **nickel**. These meteorites, including the ones to the right, are magnetic and look different from most rocks on Earth.

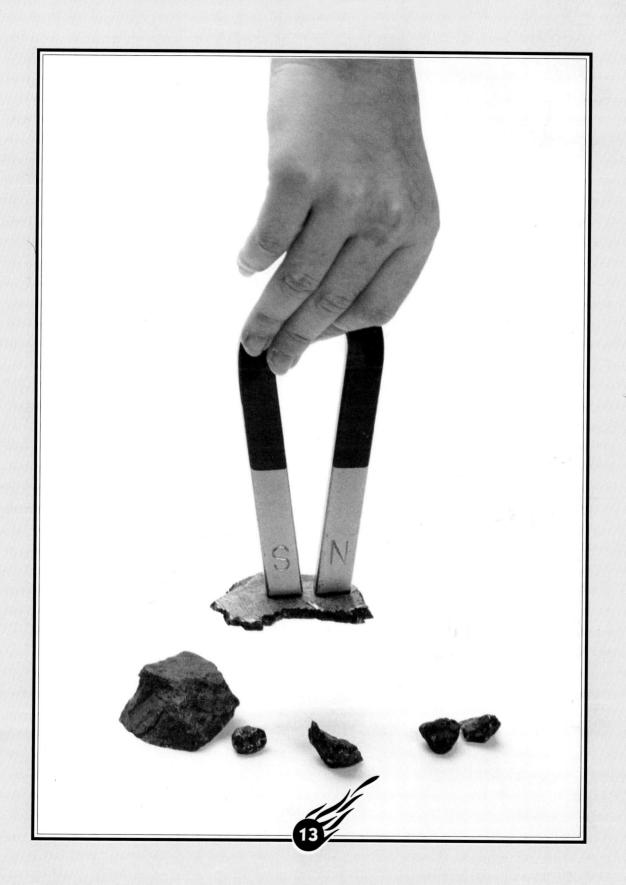

Danger — Cosmic Blasting Zone

Some meteors are rocks broken off from the Moon, other planets, or other **heavenly bodies**. For example, if a very large object collides with a planet, huge pieces of rock blast away from the planet's surface. The rocks fly into space. They may orbit the Sun for millions of years. They may swing close to Earth and eventually crash into our planet.

Scientists have found meteorites in Antarctica that came from the Moon. They have also found meteorites they think came from Mars.

Clouds of Dust

Other meteors come from **comets**. Comets
are bits of rock and dust frozen in a ball of ice.
If a comet skims near the Sun, the Sun's heat
melts the comet. After this, a cloud of dust
and rock is all that remains. Earth sometimes
passes through these dusty clouds. The dust
enters Earth's atmosphere, forming a shower
of meteors. This picture shows a spectacular
meteor shower that occurred in 1870 when
Earth passed through a cloud of dust. Meteors
swarmed in the night sky like snowflakes.

Watch the Stars, See How They Fall

On any given night, shooting stars streak across the sky. But some times of the year are better for watching shooting stars than others. Some calendars show times when meteor showers occur.

During an average meteor shower, you can see as many as sixty shooting stars in an hour! So choose a clear, moonless night when there is a meteor shower, go to a place away from streetlights, and enjoy the show.

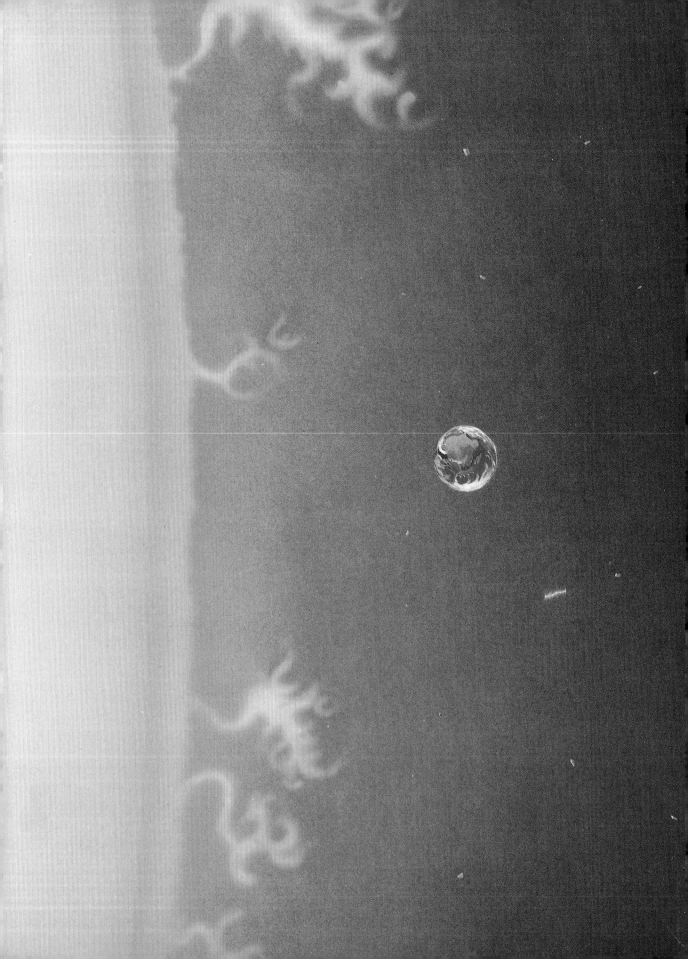

Shooting Stars — Stars That Aren't Stars

No matter how many shooting stars you spot, you will never see a real star streak by. Real stars are very different from shooting stars. They are huge, distant globes of hot gas that give off light and heat. Our Sun is a star. In this painting, you can see how huge it is compared with Earth.

Shooting stars are meteors — glowing bits of rock whizzing through Earth's atmosphere. Stars glow for billions of years, but meteors flash for only a second. Stars cannot fall to Earth, but meteors can.

The Mysteries of Meteors

We now know that shooting stars aren't stars. They are meteors. But meteors themselves contain many mysteries. Through what strange regions have they passed on their far-flung journeys? What can they tell us about distant times and places far from Earth? Our questions about meteors keep us wondering about our own world and about the fascinating mysteries of outer space.

More Books to Read

Comets and Meteors by Isaac Asimov (Gareth Stevens)
Did Comets Kill the Dinosaurs? by Isaac Asimov (Gareth Stevens)
Voyagers From Space: Meteors and Meteorites by Patricia Lauber
    (Harper & Row Junior Books)

Places to Write

Here are some places you can write to for more information about shooting stars, meteors, and meteorites. Be sure to tell them exactly what you want to know about. Give them your full name and address so that they can write back to you.

National Space Society
600 Maryland Avenue SW
Washington, D.C. 20024

Stardate
McDonald Observatory
Austin, Texas 78712

Space Communications Branch
Ministry of State for Science
    and Technology
240 Sparks Street
C. D. Howe Building
Ottawa, Ontario K1A 1A1

Glossary

atmosphere (AT-muh-sfear): the gases that surround a planet, star, or moon.

comet (KAHM-et): an object made of ice, rock, dust, and gas that orbits the Sun. When it travels near the Sun, the comet develops a tail of gases that may be seen from Earth.

crater (KRATE-er): a hole on a planet or moon gouged out by a meteorite.

heavenly body: a star, planet, moon, or other natural object that is found in space.

iron (EYE-urn): a silver or black metal that rusts in moist air; some meteorites contain iron.

meteor (MEE-tee-or): a piece of rock or dust traveling through Earth's atmosphere.

meteor shower: a period when a large number of meteors can be seen when Earth is traveling through a dust cloud in space.

meteorite (MEE-tee-or-ite): a meteor that hits Earth.

nickel (NICK-uhl): a hard, silvery metal used in making some coins; some meteorites contain nickel.

star: a huge, hot, glowing globe of gases in outer space.

Index

Antarctica 14
Arizona 10

comets 17
craters 10-11

Mars 14
Mercury 11
meteor showers 17, 18
meteorites 8, 12-15
meteors 8-9, 14-15, 21, 22
Moon 11, 14

stars 7, 21
Sun 21